GROWING IN THE GOSPEL

A PILGRIM'S JOURNEY TO DISCOVER JESUS

Finding Jesus through the original meaning of His words and actions

REVISED AND UPDATED

Michael Harvey Koplitz

Table of Contents

Introduction

The search to finding God is one that many people will take some time during their lives. You may be on that journey right now. You may be preparing to start your journey and need some guidance. Whether you have taken the journey or are starting it, this essay is about my journey and how I discovered Jesus. Why should you care about reading my journey? Of course, I will say that it is an exciting journey that will continue for the rest of my physical life and I dare say it will continue into the world to come.

In this essay, I discuss the various things that I have learned on the journey. Some of what I have discovered on the journey you may not like. Some readers will say that this essay opened their eyes to what I found. Some readers have been asking the same questions for years and have had difficulties finding the answers. Well, I can tell you I have had and still have a lot of questions. For some questions, I found the answers. For some, I will have to wait until I meet God face to face to discover the solutions.

Christianity likes to use the term "pilgrim." It is used to name a person on a spiritual quest to finding God. Many people over the centuries from all religions will take the spiritual journey.

The tricky part of the pilgrimage is that you must be ready to shed some of your beliefs. Or, in my case, I did not have a belief system in place. So, shedding it at the beginning of the journey was not an issue. However, I must tell you that you will discover in this essay that I developed a belief system that I questioned and eventually shattered for a new and what I feel is a better understanding of God.

Shedding your belief system is not a simple thing. Of course, a lot depends on how long you have held on to your truths and how many of them you are willing to let go. On your personal journey, you will hit obstacles. These items will slow you down; however, you must never let them stop you. If a doctrine that you have believed in is inconsistent, it could rattle your entire belief system. That is actually a good thing. Why? Because you are thinking about the core foundation of your belief system. As you learn and grow in faith, your belief system could change. Remember that it is a personal journey. Do not let anyone tell you anything different! That is an enormous problem that I discovered with the Church. The powers in charge want you to believe in a system that dictates what you are to believe. I fell into that system also and learned how to live within that system and how I changed my belief system based on my discoveries.

I invite you to follow in my footsteps and see what I discovered over the years of intense religious study. I will reveal a treasure house of discoveries about the Bible, church doctrine, and what I have learned about Jesus Christ. Some writers like to say "searching for the historical Jesus." That statement fits to a point what I wanted to know about. Who was Jesus, son of Joseph from the town of Nazareth? Here's the first shocker for too many readers. Jesus who lived at the beginning of the first century CE, is not the Jesus the Church espouses. Did you stop and say, "what?" Yes, I said it, and I will show you why I said it. So, do not stop reading on that account. There is a lot more to come and a lot more to shock some of you. After coming to accept Jesus as my savior, I questioned everything. As I learned more and more, I started asking more questions. Let's begin the journey, and I will add the questions that I had along the way.

So, let us go to the beginning. I was born into a non-practicing Jewish family. My parents did not have a need for religion and did not practice Judaism. This should not be surprising. There are plenty of families of all faiths who are, in name, a part of a religion. My first time in a synagogue for Sabbath worship was when my older brother (my Irish twin) was Bar Mitzvah. Training for the Bar Mitzvah was a five-year process of attending Hebrew School. It was always an embarrassment to tell the class teachers that my parents did not take part in Sabbath worship. Of course, we participated in the Rosh HaShannah and Yom

Kippur worship. That is where synagogue attendance stopped. If I counted all the times, I attended a Sabbath worship, it would be three. Two brothers and I were Bar Mitzvah. Later on, I discovered that my paternal grandparents, orthodox Jews, paid for us to go to Hebrew School. They considered a grandson who was not Bar Mitzvah a family stain, and they would not let that happen. So, my journey begun with a contradiction. Why was this Bar Mitzvah ceremony that important? As a side note, as a church pastor, I saw plenty of kids go through Confirmation and never saw them on Sunday.

I can say that religion and God were not a real part of my life at that time. I went to college and toyed with the idea of attending Sabbath worship and High Holy day worship. That desire faded quickly because there was nothing to push me toward it. I gave up that idea as fast as it came into my head.

During my senior year of college, I fell in love with a wonderful woman. She was a Christian who was a member of a local United Methodist Church. It did not matter to me she was not Jewish. In fact, the girls I dated in college who were Jewish all had some psychological problem, at least from my point of view. I did not have a "full connection" to Judaism, so her being a Christian did not matter.

When our first child was about to be born, I told my bride that she should bring up the child to know God through the Church. My religious connection to God was narrow. The children needed to learn about God. Therefore, she took our three children to Church. Yes, by herself. Many mothers take the kids to Church while dad stays at home. In my case, I was not a Christian and did not believe in Jesus Christ. Therefore, why would I go to Church to hear the pastor tell me that I would be going to hell because I was not saved? I was saved because I was one of God's Chosen People. At least, that is what five years of Hebrew School taught me.

The pastor of the UM church was brilliant. He encouraged a children's choir and had them sing during Sunday worship at least once a month. How could I say no to my three children when they asked daddy to come to hear them sing? You got it; I went to Church to listen to them sing. The pastor knew that he had non-believers in his midst and took advantage of it. However, he did not do the Baptist thing of telling me I was hell-bound. Instead, he spoke about receiving God's love by coming to know Jesus. That was a fantastic way to express the Christian religion.

When I reached thirty-five years old, I started to ponder life. I was taught as a child that the class was half empty. What that did was it gave me a negative slant on life. I did not want to have this slant. I spent some time reading about the different psychology of positive thinking and eventually religion. Christianity was the last religion I read about. My wife gave me a paraphrased Bible to read. I also read Scott Peck's book "The Road Less Traveled." Peck said that the old had to die for the new to be born. I came to understand Jesus' death and resurrection as the ancient dying and new being born. That was when I came to believe in the power of salvation through Jesus Christ. My old self had to die for my new self to be born. Eureka! I thought I discovered the keys to the kingdom. I was baptized in the UM church.

Now I wanted to learn everything I could about Jesus and Christianity. The first barrier I hit was when I was told that I could only be educated in Sunday School. I discovered that I knew more about God and the Bible than the instructor of the class. I did try a couple of different classes with the same result. How could I possibly know more than these instructors? I learned over time that anyone who could read from the assigned book and regurgitate it was allowed to be an instructor in the UM church (it is probably the same everywhere).

Then in 1997 came the two visions from God. Both dreams directed me to learn the Gospels and preach the original message of Jesus Christ. I had a tiny clue to what that truly meant at that time. The only way I learned about Jesus' message was to become a pastor in the

UM church. I needed real education, and that meant Seminary. As a pastor in the UM church, I could learn the Gospels and preach the word of God to people. That was essentially my calling. Therefore, I asked the pastor of the Church I attended to help me fulfill Jesus' calling. He did, and I was on my way to learning about Jesus! What a happy day that was.

The UM process of becoming an ordained elder of the Church is long and tedious. However, I seemed to breeze through most of it. I felt that Jesus' calling to me was being fulfilled. My ultimate goal was to learn what the Gospel message meant when Jesus spoke. As I prepared to begin Seminary life, I was convinced that the Church had the message correct. I started part-time studies at Lancaster Theological Seminary. My transition from being a Computer Engineer/Project Manager to becoming a church pastor was a two-year process.

Contradictions of Seminary and Church

Let the learning begin! I was gung ho to start Seminary. I learned quickly that there were many students in my classes at the Seminary because their denomination required it. They wanted to get their passing grade and get out as soon as possible. I, on the other hand, wanted to learn everything I could. I was like a sponge. Most of the instructors seemed annoyed at times that I would ask so many questions. Without indoctrination to the Church since infancy, I did not have the paradigms of Church in me. I wanted to know everything I could, which meant questioning what the instructors were saying. In the middle of the Seminary life, I had to do an inventory of where I was in the process. My advisor, who was not much of one, brought up this point of my asking a lot of questions. She made it sound like a bad thing. Reader beware of these people. ASK QUESTIONS!! That is how you can learn the deeper meaning of Scripture verses the doctrine that the Church espouses.

A great example of asking questions and then seeing how the church suppresses free thought can be found in the movie "Luther." A scene in the film is when Martin Luther was in his seminary classroom and raises a question. It was about the Catholic Church declaring that all saints of the Orthodox Church were invalid. To the Catholic church, saints could only be Catholic. Luther asked about the saints before the split of 1096 CE (this was when the one

Church became two – Catholic and Orthodox). Were the saints on the orthodox side of the Church before the split still saints. The answer Luther received was a question, "Was he questioning the authority of the church?" Asking questions about the Church's interpretation of the Bible or its doctrine was considered heresy at that time. In many cases, it is heresy today! This approach allows the Church to maintain the power of the beliefs of the people in Jesus. Is that what Jesus wanted? NO!

How about an examination of the Nicene creed or even the apostles' creed? God the Father begot a Son proceeded by the Holy Spirit. This is a big problem. It is called Trinity

Doctrine today. The Catholic and Protestant belief is that the Father, Son, and Spirit always existed, three in one. The Orthodox faith is that the Father and Son always existed, two in one. Then, on Easter evening, from John's Gospel, Jesus visited the disciples, created the Holy Spirit, and gave it to them. Thus, Trinity became three in one. The Nicene creed reflects the Orthodox version.

How did the Catholic Church get around this problem? In Seminary, when I questioned the language, I was told that the writers could not figure out how to write the statement to meet the needs of both sides. I was told to believe that "proceeds" indicated a different relationship and did not indicate what the

Orthodox Church believed. To think any different was heresy. Many people were burned at the stake by the Church because they questioned this wording about the Trinity. You are expected to accept this three in one idea if you want to call yourself a Christian.

Where does it say this in the Bible? That one place is at the end of Matthew's Gospel, where Jesus supposedly said, "Go out and baptize in the name of the Father, the Son, and the Holy Spirit." This is an add-on to the Gospel to meet the belief of the Proto-Orthodox Church. Later on, I will prove this by showing you that baptism is a ritual adopted from the ancient Mithras cult. A note about baptism is how many baptisms did Jesus do according to the

Gospels? Wait a minute, none. If baptism was so necessary, then why did Jesus not perform the ritual? The answer is Mithras.

This question is impossible for the Seminary or the Church to answer. If Jesus was God incarnate, then God has returned to the Earth. This is a very logical statement that is accepted by Christianity. However, the minor prophets spoke about the "Day of the LORD." This theological prophecy states that one day the LORD was going to return to the Earth. On that day, judgment would happen to all the humans left on the planet. It is described as a day of terror and hardship. The minor prophets told us to prepare ourselves for this day. One must repent of one's sins before the LORD returns.

If Jesus is truly God incarnate as the Church espouses, then what happened to the "Day of the LORD." The end of time should have arrived upon Jesus' birth. The LORD had returned. But the end of the world did not happen. The question of Jesus' divinity comes into question. The Seminary and Church through a roadblock up immediately. How dare a person question Jesus' divinity in the way the Church espouses and has espoused for two thousand years?

How can the Church answer the question about the "Day of the LORD?" The writers during that first century of Christianity developed an answer. That answer is the book of Revelation. In that book, it says that the minor prophets were not wrong about the Day of the LORD. They just missed one minor issue. The LORD will return twice. The first time as the Messiah and the second time to bring the end of time. Does this mean that Revelation trumps the minor prophets? Obviously, yes. It became difficult for the Church to recruit converts from Judaism when Christianity declared Jesus to be God. You are probably saying that Christianity always believed that Jesus was divine. That is not historically true. Several scholars have written books on this topic. Somewhere between 33 CE and 90 CE, Jesus was "made" God by the Church.

A lot of pastors in the Church have dismissed the Hebrew Scriptures (Old Testament), and by doing so, they eliminate the "Day of the LORD" question. Most Christians are not aware of this prophecy. The Hebrew Scriptures have many rules and regulations that pastors say do not apply to Christians today. They use Paul's words from Galatians that we live under grace and not the Law. Admittedly, there are a lot of antiquated laws in the Hebrew Scriptures. Indeed, the Laws about animal sacrifice at the Temple cannot be followed today. The Laws found in the Torah (the first five books) number 613. They can be divided into four categories: Love God, Love Neighbor, Being Jewish, and Temple rituals. Indeed, loving God and neighbor is essential.

Jesus called them the two great commandments. Many church pastors toss the Hebrew Scriptures out and tell us that only Jesus' way counts. Oh yes, they forgot that Jesus came to fulfill the Torah, not to toss it out.

Jesus gave us the absolute best interpretation and best way to implement the Laws that are found in the Hebrew Scriptures. He did not toss them aside. Instead, He lived by them. Many Christians like to say that they follow the way of Jesus. If they really want to do this, they must become devout Jews. I bet some readers just cringed at that statement. Big news, Jesus was a devout Jew! If you want to be like Jesus in your devotion to God, remember that Jesus was Jewish. That means that Jesus was not a Christian. That is another shocker. Jesus was Jewish. He followed the Laws of the Torah. He prayed daily with his minion (a minion is ten or more men). He did not eat bacon and certainly did not put cheese on his meat. He followed the purity and kosher laws of Leviticus. If you want to be like Jesus, then you must behave as a devout Jew.

So, where did this "Christian behavior" come from? The quick answer is from Paul the Apostle. There will be more on this later. Jesus never said to toss out the Hebrew Scriptures. In fact, he quoted it often and lived by its Laws. Why does the Church de-emphasize the Hebrew Scriptures? Why do educated pastors tell their congregations that they do not have to follow anything in the Hebrew Scriptures? At my first church appointment, I received a letter from the Senior Pastor's wife condemning me for preaching on the Hebrew Scriptures. She clearly scolded me about this and demanded that only the Gospels be preached in any Christian church. This woman had a seminary degree but never used it. Her husband only preached on gospel passages. This sends a message to the congregation that even Paul's letters are not valuable.

If the Hebrew Scriptures are not to be followed or preached, why did Lancaster Theological Seminary require three courses in the Hebrew Scriptures? The bottom line is that these pastors are wrong! The Hebrew Scriptures were placed into the Bible because they are sacred documents. The Church dealt with the Hebrew Scriptures problem at the beginning. The Montanist movement said that the God of the Hebrew Scriptures was not the God of Jesus. Therefore, they only followed the Christian Scriptures (the New Testament). The Proto-Orthodox Church called them heretics and destroyed their movement. Thus, the Church says that the Hebrew Scriptures are essential. The Church expressed through its pastors has a different message about the value of the Hebrew Scriptures.

Let us connect the Bible to Church doctrine. When you learn about church doctrine from the Seminary or the Church, both will tell you that Church doctrine is biblically based. Was the original development of a doctrine biblically based? Not every time. One example is why Catholic priests are forbidden to marry? The Church imposed this doctrine at the beginning of feudalism. In that societal structure, property was passed down from father to the first-born son.

A feudal lord of a manor had serfs working in the fields. The lord would request that a church building be placed on his land and a priest assigned. He would give enough for the priest's family to survive and to send some of the money earned to the Vatican in Rome. However, when the priest died, his property was inherited by the first-born son. This included the church building, and property. The feudal lord lost the Church that he had built for his serfs. More importantly, to the Church it lost the income from that Church. How did the Church solve this problem? Easy, a doctrine was declared that priests could not be married. It should be added that only legitimate first-born sons could inherit property. Therefore, when the priest died, the property remained under the Vatican's control.

When Feudalism ended, this doctrine was unnecessary. However, the Catholic Church loves tradition over Scripture. This doctrine had become a tradition and had been in place for hundreds of years. Since the Church will not end a useless doctrine, it changed the basis of the doctrine into a biblical calling. Paul said in his letters that he would not marry and bring children into the world. Paul's reason was that he believed Jesus was to return before the end of his life. Therefore, he had to spend all his days warning people about Christ's return. Paul had no time for a family. He also believed that one should not spend time on family when preparing themselves for judgment day. The Catholic Church could easily change this doctrine and resolve a lot of its clergy problems. However, traditions are vital in the Church. Perhaps one day, the change will be made.

A more profound doctrine to fathom is Augustine's doctrine of Original Sin. This doctrine has been with the Church since around 400 CE. Did you know children were not baptized before 400 CE? Probably you did not, unless you read some "liberal" history books on Christianity? The Church does not want you to know this. Why? Augustine's doctrine, in a nutshell, is that the sin of Adam and Eve is passed down through the generations by procreation. Therefore, every baby is born with the sin of Adam and Eve, the Original Sin. They must be baptized immediately so that Jesus can protect them. Creating this false narrative about a child being sinful because the parents created the child through sex allowed the Church to control parents. The Church scared the parents to baptize the child. This doctrine is a doctrine of control.

Augustine said that Satan was in the Garden of Eden and forced Eve to eat from the Tree of Good and Evil. This is a false narrative. The Bible says that a crafty snake caused Eve to eat from the Tree. There is a Midrash about this incident that I will briefly offer here. Snakes originally had legs and arms just like humans. The snake in the Garden wanted to eliminate the humans to become the favored animal of God and thus take the place of the humans. The Midrash also says that Adam told Eve that if she touched the tree, she would die. He was trying to keep Eve away from it.

One day, Eve was next to the tree. The snake came up to her and said that she should eat the fruit of the tree. Eve explained God said do not do this, and Adam told her to stay away from it because just touching it meant death. The snake pushed Eve into the tree. She felt the tree and did not die. The snake then told Eve that she was lied to and would not die if she ate the fruit. So, she ate the fruit and did not die (well, not immediately). Midrash continues as the Genesis story.

Satan was not in the Garden. There is a question whether Satan was even "created" yet. If you read the Book of the Watchers from 1 Enoch (chapters 1 to 36) you will learn when Satan came to be. Satan's creation does not occur until chapter six of Genesis. Therefore, Satan could not have been in the Garden. Hence, Augustine's doctrine of original sin has no biblical basis. Yes, you read that correctly. Original sin, which the Church has been telling followers for sixteen centuries, is not biblically based. There are more church doctrines like this one. As I learned about the various church doctrines and their true origins, I questioned their validity.

The Church's history is full of opportunities for it to have power over people. The Vatican is a wealthy nation today. How many thousands of dollars are in the Pope's robes? Probably enough to feed an entire Latin American country for a year. I sat in a Catholic church in Aquapretta, Mexico, which had a hole in its roof. During the Sunday worship, a special collection was taken to send to the Vatican. Why did the Vatican expect money from this poor church instead of telling it to fix its roof? I will leave that question for you to contemplate.

To find Jesus, peel back the Church doctrine, which is defining Jesus and the church with no original biblical support. It is hard to do this if you have been indoctrinated in the ways of the Church for a long time.

Ancient Bible Study Methods

As I continued my first seminary degree, the Master of Divinity, the more I learned about the workings of the Church and the way the Church interpreted the Bible. What this did was to raise more questions about both. The interpretations of Scripture being forced down my throat by seminary instructors did not match what the actual Scripture said. Schools, colleges, and seminaries teach using the Greek Method. Basically, this method, which was developed by Aristotle, states that the teacher is the expert, and the student must absorb as told. There is no room for deep questioning of the expert. The Church moved early in its history from Jerusalem to Rome. When that happened, the Church lost its Hebraic style of learning and picked up the Greek method. The Jewish members of the Church dwindled. The Gentiles filled the Church and brought their Greek learning method with them. Therefore, today to question the teacher, considered the expert, is not acceptable.

In Seminary, in the Old Testament class, the instructor spent three hours lecturing about how the prophets do not predict the coming of Jesus Christ. Lancaster Theological Seminary would be considered a liberal religious institution. That lecture did not sit well with the class. The class was instructed to write a reflection paper on the topic. It did not matter whether I agreed with the instructor; I wrote a paper regurgitating everything she said. The documents were handed back to us after a week. A couple of students from that class were in the library when poor Fred came in crying about the "F" he received on his reflection paper. He had always been a straight "A" student. His paper was titled "The Prophets Do predict Jesus." It was a difficult pill for Fred to swallow, but he learned you must agree with the instructor in the Greek Method of learning; after all, she was the expert. So, he rewrote the paper and got his "A." I learned this lesson in my undergraduate work. The instructors wanted the students to think; however, they wanted correct thinking: their way of thinking, which was their way.

The Greek Method of learning works very well for the Church, which wants to control your religious life. Question nothing is the motto of the Church education system. After observing Sunday School class for over twenty years, amateurs clearly used the Greek Method too. Why not? That is the way they learned.

Not being allowed to question what the instructor, the pastor, the bishop said is Christianity's hallmark. The more I learned about the Bible, Christian history, and Christian Doctrine, the more I questioned things. I read a lot of writings outside of the direct control of the Church to find the answers. For example, Jesus' parables are the finest parables ever written. The problem is that they made little sense. I searched for explanations for the parables for years. The usual answer I received was what the Church says it means and be satisfied with that.

Well, that would not work. I did not know but I rejected the Greek method of learning while I was not accepting the standard church explanation of the parables. I purchased a book written by Dr. Anne Davis about the parables. This author was different! She asked the questions about the parables that I was asking. Instead of being told to be quiet and accept the Church's position, Dr. Davis explained the parables in a new way. I had to speak with this lady about her method. So, I called the organization BibleInteract that she was with.

We had a great conversation, and I discovered she put together the information I knew in a beautiful package, which allowed me to learn to discover the original meaning of Jesus' words.

That was my calling from Jesus!!! Just a quick review. Jesus told me to learn the original meaning of His words and preach it to the world. I had to learn everything the Church was saying and doing because this forced me to keep searching. I finally found a mentor who demanded that I ask more questions. This is the Hebraic way of learning. Greek learning was to narrow the conversation to what the expert said. The Hebraic learning method is to open the dialogue as broadly as possible by asking questions about everything. Hallelujah!

Dr. Davis calls her method, which is mine now, Ancient Bible Study Methods. It is a modernization of the biblical learning methods developed by the Sage Hillel. This sage lived about 70 years before Jesus' birth. He brought the Hebraic method of learning and study into biblical studies. The day of the Great Assembly was over, and Hillel's school taught that having only one opinion of interpreting Scripture was incorrect. Ask questions about everything was Hillel's mantra. When you examine the Jewish understanding of the Bible, there are numerous volumes of books. Each interpretation by each sage or rabbi has one thing in common: it raises more questions. The Sages said that there are at least 70 interpretations of the Torah. A devout Jew attending Sabbath worship will hear the Torah read at least 70 times (during a "normal" life span today). People repeat the Torah every year. Therefore, there are at least 70 understandings. Each learning is supposed to raise unanswered questions for the following year. Learning NEVER ENDS in the Hebraic method.

You can learn the details of the method with my additions by visiting my website, http://michaelkoplitz.info, or BibleInteract's website, http://bibleinteract.com, or by purchasing my book on Ancient Bible Study Methods. I will now explore two areas that added to Dr. Davis' original model, which I believe will help you discover Jesus as I did.

The first is language. To fully understand the Bible, the original language must be examined. However, most Christians do not speak Hebrew, Aramaic, and Koine Greek has not been a spoken language in 1800 years. The best way to examine the original languages of the Bible is to use a computer software program. Currently, I am using Accordance Bible software. There is an exciting nuance when examining the Gospels. The most significant point is that the Gospels were written in Koine Greek, but Jesus spoke Hebrew and Aramaic. Since Hebrew was considered a religious language and spoken mainly in the Temple at

Jerusalem and synagogues, Jesus would have spoken Aramaic. Also, being from Galilee, he probably spoke the Galilean dialect of Aramaic.

In Dr. Davis' model, she examines the Koine Greek for her interpretations of the New Testament. I do the same thing, but I also look at the Peshitta (the Aramaic New Testament). I also use an Aramaic commentary series written by Dr. Errico Rocco and Dr. George Lamsa. Hebrew and Aramaic words rarely change meaning. The terms may vary in their usage but not their meaning. For example, English has changed over the past 300 years. If you are reading a King James Version of the Bible, you are reading words, in many cases, that have changed or are obsolete. The famous verse I use to show the difference is "Jesus said, suffer the children to come to me." Suffer? 300 years ago, the word suffer meant let and let meant suffer. These two words switched meanings. Therefore, the verse today reads, "Jesus said, Let the children come to me." The New King James Bible will contain modern English. If you insist on using this Bible, then please use the new one. The other complication with the King James Bible is that the Old Testament was based on the Vulgate. The Vulgate Bible is a Latin translation of the Septuagint Bible. The Septuagint is the Greek translation of the Hebrew Scriptures. The King James Bible has passed through several translations. When translations are done, the nuances of the original language are usually lost.

Learning about Jesus' words in Aramaic will get you closer to the original meaning. Hebrew and Aramaic are languages that were developed upon the culture of the day. Words are derived from root words. An example is the root word for "word" (*dabar* in Hebrew). Therefore, anything that contained words uses a derivative of *dabar*. The word for a sentence and paragraph are clear examples. The word for Law is a derivative of *dabar* because the Law is a collection of words.

Another example is *ruach*. This word can mean "Spirit of God", "your spirit," "breath," or "wind." The Spirit of God, which some call the Shekinah, moves through the world. You cannot see the *Ruach* (Spirit of God), but you can see the results. The wind is the same. You cannot see it, but you can definitely see its effects.

The nuances of the original meaning of Jesus' words are found in the Aramaic version, the Peshitta. There are English versions of the Peshitta. Since Aramaic is closely connected to the culture, a commentary series on culture is vital. Dr. Rocco's commentary relates the Aramaic version of the New Testament with the culture of the day. He has also developed commentaries using the Aramaic language for the Old Testament. There are good books written by researchers about the culture of Jesus' day that is available to you. The exciting thing about the culture of the Near East is that much of it has not changed. Additions have occurred because of modern times. Near Eastern people treasure past customs and remain a part of their lives today.

When I was in Seminary, I asked the Old Testament instructor about a series of writings I learned about called the Targums. She immediately dismissed the Targums as useless, and she never studied them. With a PhD in the Old Testament, I would have thought the Targums would have been reviewed. Some readers are wondering what the Targums are. They are the Aramaic translations of the

Hebrew Scriptures with one significant additional feature. The translators added words to the verses to offer an understanding of the verse. The creators of the Targum did this because so many Jews in 200 CE did not live in Judea or Galilee, and it was thought that they could not read Hebrew. So, they used Aramaic to get the Bible into the hands of the Jewish people. They explained the customs of the day in the Targum. If you are going to study anything from the Old Testament, you really need the appropriate Targum. Targums are available in English for just about every Old Testament book. One major exception is Daniel. A surprise too many readers will be that Daniel is about one-half Hebrew and one-half Aramaic. A Targum was never written for Daniel.

Learning the culture of Jesus' day is imperative to fully understand His message. Jesus used examples from His culture in just about everything He said. Some things did not have to be written because it was common knowledge. A modern example would say in your diary that you went to church on Sunday. You would not describe how you got there, a car with gas, a driver's license, and more. The same goes for the writers of the Gospels. They did not write what was clear to the people of their day. Therefore, there is a lot of "missing information." It is not missing because the people of Jesus' day knew their culture. You must fill in a lot of information to get the original meaning of Jesus' words, thus finding Jesus!

Another critical aspect of the culture of Jesus' day is that Hebraic storytelling differs greatly from our Greek-based storytelling. There are four stories about what happened on Easter morning in the Gospels. Detractors of Christianity say that since the stories are different, the event did not occur. They believe this because they do not understand storytelling in the Near East, especially in Jesus' day. The four stories about the resurrection are the same story. Hebraic storytelling is not about the story but the message of the story. The core idea or event being explained is the key. Jesus' tomb was empty because God raised Him from the dead. Everything else is what I call window dressing. It is material that creates a superb story and frankly does not matter to the Near Easterner.

The same holds true for the birth narrative in Luke's Gospel. The message is that Jesus the Messiah was born in Bethlehem. All the fanfare and angels are just a part of good storytelling. This story probably started as a simple story with Mary and Joseph in Bethlehem, like in Matthew's story, then over the years until it was written the story because more intense. It is like the story of the fishers who caught a six-inch fish on the lake. By the time he got home, it was a six-foot monster fish. The message of the story is that he caught a fish. The rest is window dressing.

If you want to get close to the original meaning of Jesus' words, you will want to use Ancient Bible Study Methods with the Aramaic language and culture of Jesus' day.

Signs and Miracles

See what happens if you ask the pastor of your church about Jesus healing people and did the signs and miracles. The snap answer will be "absolutely yes." I believed that too when I started my journey. I learned about a couple of things along the way, and I offer it as speculation. Could Jesus have cured people and turned water into wine? Yes, I believe He could have and did. Did He do this through divine will? That is another question.

In the book "Mary a Flesh and Blood Biography of the Virgin Mother" written by Lesley Hazleton, the author researched the question about Jesus' healing. What she discovered was Anna, Mary's mother, and

Mary were healers. The two women were midwives by trade. In Jesus' day, midwives also functioned as physicians. They knew how the various plants could create cures for many diseases. The author believes Mary taught Jesus the trade. It was a secret trade that could only be obtained by someone teaching it to you. If he was taught the midwives' healing ways, then He was curing people with that knowledge. There was no divinity involved in these healings. But do not forget about Hebraic storytelling. The central message of Jesus' healing story is that Jesus healed the diseased person. Everything else is window dressing.

The Hebraic storyteller would add to the glory and fantasy of a story to capture his/her audience. What a dull story it would be about Jesus healing a person if it does not have a lot of fanfare. The first Gospel is probably Mark (some scholars believe in an earlier document named "Q" existed). If you compare equal stories from Mark and Matthew, you will discover a lot of Hebraic storytelling in Matthew. Mark was probably written in the early 60s CE. That was thirty years after Jesus' life. That is plenty of time to create the window dressing.

To discover the original meaning of Jesus' actions, the Hebraic storytelling must be removed. When this is done, the message of the story is revealed. A fundamental message of Jesus' healing is that He loved people and healed them. He never asked for money or any compensation for his healing. He wanted to heal people. He loved His neighbor. Remember, early on, I said that Jesus was a devout Jew. So, if you want to be like Jesus, love your neighbor as Jesus did. Jesus loved Jews and Gentiles alike. He showed no partiality to one group over another.

A Near Eastern culture was for disciples to write books about their rabbis. I learned about his cultural item from Rabbi Steinsaltz while reading his book titled "The Strife of the Spirit." He said that the disciples of Rabbi Isaac Luria, also known as the Ari (which means lion in Hebrew) wrote a book called the "Tales of the Ari." In this book, the disciples wrote about how the Ari could heal people and perform signs and miracles. It did not matter if the Ari did anything described in the tales. What mattered was that the Ari's disciples were so enamored with him they created a book about him. It makes the Ari seem bigger than life, almost divine.

So did Jesus' disciples love their rabbi so much that they created books about Him doing signs and miracles? If you examine the Gospels in this manner, and there are other Gospels about Jesus, the answer is yes. Again, considering Hebraic storytelling, one can see how the stories from the disciples and original followers of Jesus enhanced the beauty of their story. It is easier to remember a person in story form than it is to remember a list of their accomplishments. A good example is the Gospel of Thomas. It is a listing of 100+ Jesus' sayings. If you read the Gospel of Thomas and then write down the Jesus sayings, how many do you think you could remember? Instead, the Gospels are Jesus' sayings with the addition of Hebraic storytelling.

Paul spoke about milk and meat when learning about Jesus. The milk person is a beginner. When I started to read the Gospel, I was told to believe every word. Therefore, every story is 100% genuine and executed in the manner it was written. To move to meat means to see the underlying spiritual lessons of the stories. Is it necessary to you that Jesus performed signs and miracles? If you say yes, you are probably still drinking milk. If not, you are either on meat or an unbeliever. Look for the spiritual awareness and lesson in the signs and miracles and every Jesus story.

Jesus opens our eyes to the spiritual connection we need with God. So, does it matter if He performs the signs and miracles as written? That is a question that you have to answer for yourself. The spiritual implications of the healing are what matters and will bring you closer to Jesus.

Divinity?

Now for a more difficult question. This question is a part of a person's journey in Christianity. Was Jesus God incarnate? Early I spoke about the question of Trinity, and if Jesus was God, why did the "Day of the LORD" not be invoked? Questioning Jesus' divinity is considered heretical by the Church. How dare anyone pose that Jesus' is not God? Is that what you think? If you are thinking in a Greek learning method, the answer is "yes" and without a doubt. If you are questioning the statement that Jesus was God incarnate, you are thinking in the Hebraic learning method.

Let us start at the beginning of the Universe. The Zohar (the mystical writings of Judaism) and the Book of Creation tell us about how God created the Universe. This process began with God needing to contract Himself to provide a space to place the known Universe and Heaven. So, space was made, and the Light of God (referred to as the uhr of Ein Sof by Kabbalists) entered. The Light of God is caused what science calls the "Big Bang." One can say that we are God dust. The energy of God was so intense that it exploded into matter. That matter is God dust. Over time the dust settled, and the Heavens and Earth were created. Scientists like to call us Star Dust. They do this because they believe that only Hydrogen and Helium were produced at the beginning. The stars formed, lived for some time, then exploded, which created the heavier elements. Whether or not that is the process is not crucial to this discussion. If we are stardust and the stardust came from the power of God, then we are made of God dust. Thus, every one of us is divine. Some of us, like the prophets, could communicate with God, while most of us cannot.

Jesus could communicate with God. He was also willing to do everything that God instructed Him to do. He brought God's message of love, hope, and grace to an evil world. The leaders of that evil world killed Him because of the message. That was very common to do in ancient times. Many prophets died bringing the message God wanted to be brought to the leaders of the Chosen People. Jesus was 100% following all of God's ordinances and commands. Thus, God raised Him from the dead.

On the third day after He died, the women came to the tomb. Their main purpose was not wanting to anoint the body, some stories say this. Rather, they were performing their custom. That custom was on the third day it was believed that the deceased soul was ready to leave the body and travel to the next world. On that day, in the morning, one could offer their final fare well. So, the women came to the tomb to say goodbye to their rabbi, Jesus. Imagine their surprise when His body was gone. Even more surprising was their seeing

Jesus! By following everything that God placed in the Torah, and the commands God gave to Jesus, He was allowed on resurrection day to be seen by His followers. According to the New Testament, Jesus stayed with His disciples for forty days. Forty is a number used in the Scripture to show readiness. After forty days, Jesus believed His disciples were ready to be on their own. So the Messiah prophet returned to God

God's divine energy created Jesus. God's divine energy also created us. Therefore, each human can say they contain divinity. The expression of that divinity is shown by how well we follow God's Law, as expressed in the Old Testament and shown to us by Jesus in the

Gospels. If one can love God and love neighbor as Jesus, just think about how much more a person could do. God has given us free will to decide what will be done with God's gift of life.

Jesus' resurrection and appearance to His disciples and followers are proof that what He preached was indeed from God. Thus, following the Gospels' examples, one would get closer to God and their own individual divinity. That is a tall order and one that few people have entirely obtained.

So, is Jesus divine? Yes. We are all a part of God. We live in a space that is surrounded by God. It is the Light of God, His energy, that keeps the Universe alive and running smoothly. Jesus was a beacon in a sinful world. He shined with the Light of God to illuminate the errors of humanity. God gave us free will and knew that humanity was going to mess up.

Why would God create us, thus making us a part of His divinity when He knew that free will would allow us to screw it up? There is a midrash that the Torah (as a Spirit) came to God before creation and wanted humans to be removed from its pages. The spirit of the Torah told God that if He creates humans and gives them freewill that they would disobey. God assured the Torah that He was aware of the problem and had built repentance and forgiveness into the fabric of the Torah. Since

God used the Torah to create the world repentance and forgiveness of sin is a part of the fabric. Forgiveness for sin is an integral part of the Universe.

Messiahship?

Is Jesus the Messiah? This question is one you will have to answer for yourself. Rabbi Steinsaltz said that each of us has to create our own Torah. I believe he meant that each of us can believe parts of the Torah. However, we must have a reason for ignoring aspects if asked by God. Another consideration is that our own Torah is how we view and how we value it. Think about Jesus as Messiah. Each person needs to determine what Messiahship means and how it affects them.

There were several messianic beliefs in the ancient world. There were also many people recognized as the messiah. One task of the

Messiah is to bring the lost back to God. The lost are people who believed in God and strayed away or people who just never believed. I call Jesus my personal Messiah. I never had a strong connection with God when I was young. However, I remember a large amount of what I learned in Hebrew School.

I strayed entirely from God when I went to college. God was not a part of my life at that point. I was on my own without parental support, financially or mentally. I felt alone. I worked full time to pay for college because my parents refused to help me, but that is a separate story. Even during the early years of my marriage, I did not have a reliance on God. The township mayor officiated my wedding.

The Messiah is supposed to bring people back to God. No matter what I now believe about the life and ministry of Jesus, I can say that He is definitely my Messiah. Learning about Jesus has brought me back to God. As I work on a commentary or writing like this one, I feel a stronger bond with God. Jesus is a part of that bond because His words and actions brought me back to God. Jesus was my path. He said the only way to the Father is through the Son. I know what He originally meant because this was a cultural statement. Still, spiritually, Jesus said I will bring you back into communion with God and He did.

I returned to God with such a passion that Jesus called me to learn the Gospels' original meaning and preach it. What a powerful message that was. That is all I must be concerned about. He is my Messiah.

Do you view Jesus as your Messiah? Some people lived before and after Jesus, who were called Messiah. Perhaps a question to entertain is why cannot God send multiple Messiahs? When Judas Maccabee and his army defeated the Seleucid's and Judea became a free nation, the people hailed him as the Messiah. He freed the country and returned the throne to a descendant of David. From the messianic tradition of his day, he was the messiah. The annual celebration of Chanukah reminds Jews of that time when the Messiah came to restore the kingdom.

Unfortunately, the restoration of Judea was short-lived, and one hundred years later, the Romans moved into Judea, and the country became a slave to the Roman Empire. At the 135 CE Second Jewish Revolt, the leader Bar Kokhba was named the Messiah. Even though the second revolt was lost and Jerusalem was utterly destroyed, the people viewed him as a messiah. So, who is your Messiah, and what did he do to become it?

Then comes the question about Jesus being the Messiah, who offers salvation. Using church language, this is called "Atonement theology."

It addresses the question I had for years and that is, "How does a man dying on a piece of wood 2000 years ago offer forgiveness for sins?" I even wrote a booklet on what I called "Born Again Theology" based on John chapter three. You may believe in "Substitution Theology." This theology is Jesus died in your place because sin requires a living sacrifice.

The ancient Hebrew people would offer animal sacrifices for sin. The sinner brought his animal to a priest at the Temple in Jerusalem. The priest would "transfer" the person's sins to the animal. The animal was then killed for the sin. Substitute theology works this way, but it is Jesus who is the cosmic sacrifice for everyone. Why did animal sacrifice begin? A Midrash tells the story that when Adam and Eve sinned, they decided that being naked was bad. So, God fashioned clothing from them. Where did God get the materials? He killed an animal and turned its skin into a leather material and fashioned the clothing. Therefore, since God killed an animal to make the clothing, sacrificing an animal for sin became real. Substitution theology extends the animal sacrifice system without the death.

You may not be aware that the Christian-Jews in Judea and Galilee brought their animal sacrifices for sin to the Temple at Jerusalem until its destruction forty years later. Therefore, Jesus was not viewed as a cosmic sacrifice for sin until after 70 CE. That Jesus died on the cross, just like many prophets did before him.

Does Jesus save you and me from sin? Absolutely yes. When Moses climbed Mount Sinai to receive the Torah from God, he was given three Torahs. The first one was the written word. The second one was the oral Law, which eventually is written and is called the Mishnah. The third one was the secret law. It was this secret law that was lost over the centuries between Moses and Jesus. Thus, Jesus brought us the secret Torah, which was lost. The Proto-orthodox Church immediately rejected this idea and called it a heresy. It was the basic premise of the Gnostic Christians.

Here is the secret law. Love God and love neighbor. That is it. Jesus called the secret law the two Great Commandments. The sage Hillel said that he could teach anyone the Torah while standing on one leg. Hillel said that the essence of the Hebrew Scripture is to love God and love neighbor. He also said everything else is commentary. Jesus said the secret to get into Heaven is to love God and love neighbor. He then showed how to do this and was recorded into the Gospels.

If you want to be forgiven for your sins, you need to follow Jesus' formula. Love God, love neighbor, repent of your sins and stop sinning. Period!

Mithras' Influence and Paul

You may want to read my book titled "Christianity's Need for Mithras." How did Christianity spread so quickly once Paul got involved? My theory (and other scholars agree) is that the Paul house churches were converted to Mithras house churches. The Mithras religion was around for a long time, even earlier than Judaism. It started in Egypt with the worship of Osiris and Ra. When it moved into the Greek world, it became the Dionisis cult. When the Persians picked it up, the movement became Mithras. This cult's god had many names. Ancient people, other than Jews, changed their alliance to a God almost as fast as people today change their underwear. However, the rituals of the cult stayed the same. Therefore, it was easy for Paul to convert Mithra's house churches.

Paul said that he always went to the synagogues first. No debate there. However, he usually got an inadequate response. When the Messiah returned, the Romans were to be destroyed, and the nation would reform and have a descendant of David on its throne. That did not happen, so how could pious Jews accept Jesus of Nazareth as the Messiah, much less as God? Therefore, Paul when to the Mithras house churches. They listened to Paul's obviously convincing argument and became Jesus' house churches. But when Paul left, he had no Scripture to leave behind, nor instructions. Books were hand copied, and he certainly did not have any. Therefore, I believe he "crossed out the name Mithras and inserted the name Jesus" in their cult definition documents. The Jesus house church followed its original rituals and prayers with the names Father, Son, and Spirit instead of the Mithras names.

Mithras was believed to be the son of God, who came to save people from their sin by dying a horrible death. Does this sound familiar? Right, that is exactly what the Church says happened, but it was Jesus and not Mithras who died for the sins of the people. With the Proto-Orthodox Church gaining speed, it could squash every Christian competitor. Groups like the Gnostics, the Ebionites, and

Marcionites were called heretics and were destroyed. The only writings we have from these groups are from the Gnostics. They buried their Gospels in an old Alexandrian garbage dump and were discovered in 1948 CE.

Mithras came into the world through a virgin birth. The initiation ritual for Mithras converts was baptism. Even communion as we know it today is from Mithras. The culture of the Near East saw this ritual differently. When Jesus held the Last Supper, He wanted an ultimate commitment from His disciples. He was asking those who took the bread to swear an allegiance to Him and His cause by breaking the bread and sharing it. The wine was to tell the disciples that commitment would not be safe or easy. That is why the Judas' betrayal is actually worse than the Gospels say. Judas made an ultimate commitment to Jesus and then turned around and broke it. In the ancient world, that was an unacceptable thing to do.

You can find articles on the internet which bring together a lot of the Church's rituals and beliefs with their Mithras counterparts. Paul's letters appear to be answers to questions from the churches about maintaining their old Mithras ethical system. Paul left the Church with an adjusted ethos. For example, virgin and child sacrifices were strictly forbidden in the new Jesus house church. The sexual immorality of the Mithras was also abolished. Yet, churches still questioned it.

A significant question for Paul is why? How did Paul go from someone who hunted down Jews who believed in the rabbi Jesus of Nazareth to become his most prominent supporter in spreading the word? The second question is why did Paul select the Mithras' house churches? Perhaps Paul realized they would be the easiest to convert. He was correct.

When did the Mithras church meet for worship? Sundays. The earliest churches met on Saturday, the Sabbath day. The Mithras church met on Sundays. That is why today's

Church worships on Sunday. How about December 25 as Jesus' birthday? Scholars agree Jesus was not born on that date. However, an important person was born that day, or at least what the Mithras house churches believed. Mithras was supposedly born on December 25. When the substitution was made, Jesus' birthday became December 25.

The concept of bishops came from Paul. He called them overseers. To ensure that his converted Mithras churches did not fall back into Mithras' hands, he assigned particular persons to watch the Church. He called them overseers. The Greek word for overseers becomes Episcopal in English, and thus Paul has burdened the Church with this hierarchy.

Judaism does not have a top-level organization to keep the synagogues together. Jewish stories are Jewish, and all synagogues follow them. Perhaps synagogues did not need a higher hierarchy because all Jewish groups believe in the idea of being God's Chosen People through the events of Egypt, Sinai, and Israel. Jews are a nation all to themselves.

Paul knew outside forces kept together Mithras house churches. He had to believe that by forcing them to work together, they would grow and prosper. On this account, he was correct.

Pagan Inclusions

Pagan inclusions into Christianity have muddied up the waters over the centuries for one trying to discover Jesus. Christian growth came from including people and nations. This inclusion was done by absorbing many of the rituals and ideas of the pagan religion. Are you surprised at this statement? Let us start with the most famous inclusion, the evergreen tree. These plants cannot grow in the Near East, at least not naturally. Therefore, the emerging Proto-orthodox Church absorbed the evergreen tree. This was a symbol of the god of the northern peoples in Scandinavia. Today it is accepted as a symbol of Christmas. It became justified by the Church saying that it represents the life that never dies because the tree does not turn brown.

I do not believe that wreaths are originally from the Near East. This is a short list of these inclusions, and there are plenty more:

1. Christmas Tree
2. Poinsettias
3. Missel Toe
4. Wreaths
5. Easter Lillies
6. Easter Eggs/Easter Bunny

A far question is, has Christian become pagan? Since these items are not in the Bible, this is a legitimate question. There are plenty of doctrines and rituals that the Church espouses that are not biblical.

To find Jesus you may have to remove these objects.

The Unity That Never Was

Unity was a top priority for Jesus. How can one preach to love God and love neighbor and not preach unity? To love one's neighbor is the foundational stone to unity. The Church has never been united and never will be (unfortunately). The disunity began when the first church council was called in 48 CE. Paul and Peter had different views of what Christianity was to be. The two worked out an arrangement. Basically, Paul got everything that he wanted. As soon as the council was over, Paul converted Mithras House churches and completely ignored Peter.

The Church at Jerusalem, which Peter established, faded into history around 90 CE. No one is sure what happened to it. It just closed and disappeared. Paul called for his churches to help the Jerusalem church, but it would appear that the help never came. The division in the Proto-Orthodox church grew, and when the Church became the only Church, Emperor Constantine made Christianity the religion of the Empire. The first thing that he noticed was that the Church was severely divided. It was divided on theological lines and who had the power? Constantine helped little when he moved the center of the Church from Rome to Constantinople, which he established in Turkey.

In 325 CE, Constantine ordered a church council to settle several divisions, especially the Trinity doctrine crisis. Was the Father, Son, and Spirit always together from the beginning of "God's time" or was the Spirit created on Easter evening? The Latin-speaking church directly opposed the Greek-speaking church. Just the fact that two different languages represented the Church was a sign of deep division. In Nicea, in 325 CE, the bishops of the Church came to the special meeting to determine Trinity doctrine. They did such a bang-up job that Nicea II was held to do it all again fifty years later. The unity around Trinity doctrine never occurred. In 1096 CE, the Orthodox part of the Church separated from the Catholic Church. Indeed, Jesus must have wept that day as when He was in the Garden of Gethsemane, praying for unity and strength for his disciples.

In 1517 CE, Martin Luther led the division of the Catholic Church. The tyranny of the Popes caused the Reformation in Rome. The church became a powerhouse, especially during the Dark ages from the fall of the Roman Empire through 1000 CE. The Church in Western Europe controlled the lives of millions of people, and after 500 years, a lot of its power was gone. The Protestant Church emerged.

In my pastoral career, I attempted to create a bond between two United Methodist churches three times. The people of each Church resisted the idea of working with another church. The thought caused factions of the Church to either leave or to fight the idea tooth and nail. The United Methodist church was founded on the idea of churches working together for the common good. Every year, each Conference holds an annual meeting of church leaders. The cry for unity is loud and clear. However, at the local church level, the cry is the opposite. Unity is something that does not exist, even within a denomination. One Church might help another, but when you talk about coming together and creating one church with multiple campuses, the cry against it is intense. Some churches have multiple campuses. Usually, it is because the Church grew into multiple campuses, or one church took over another church. Therefore, it is not a merger or a union; it is a takeover.

Jesus must be weeping every time He sees His churches, not willing to come together for the greater good. The idea of unity is false.

Today's Mainline Churches

Jesus did not want to build a new religious organization. I can say this because there is no place in the Gospels where he says this. He wanted reform for the Jewish people and inclusion for the Gentiles. A Midrash talks about the Jewish people receiving God's Torah at Mount Sinai and then spreading it into the world. The Jewish people did not have the time to spread the word of God because of the persecution that the people endured since the time of Abraham, Isaac, and Jacob. There were always enemies who wanted to destroy God's people. It has been through the grace of God that the Jewish nation has survived.

Jesus wanted the mission of spreading God's Law to happen. Therefore, He spent time with Samaritans and other non-Jewish people, letting them know God loved them too. The church narrative that the Hebrew people rejected Jesus, therefore, he went to the Gentiles, is a false narrative. The Church created it to prop itself as being a part of God's plan. What many Christians do not know is that Judaism was a popular religion in Jesus' day. Proselytes were plenty. The Gentiles read the words of the prophets. The proof of this is the magi who see the Bethlehem star and journey over 1000 miles to meet Jesus when He was born. That was a lengthy and expensive trip for the three men. The spiritual meaning of the story is to tell the world that God wanted the world to know His word.

But then came Paul, and the narrative changed. The Church that we have today is the brainchild of Paul. As he went throughout the Roman Empire, he converted Mithras house churches into Jesus' house churches. He separated the Proto-orthodox Church from Judaism at the 48 CE council. Members of his Church did not have to go through the conversion to Judaism process as people did in the Jerusalem church. Paul clearly tells us in his letters that his newly founded churches were not to be a part of the established religion called Judaism. He brought the morality of Judaism to the Mithras followers and the Hebrew Scriptures, but that was it.

The idea of popes and bishops was not an idea that Jesus ever mentioned. Jesus' ideas for the reformation of Judaism did not include an additional hierarchy. Jesus knew that if a hierarchy was created in Judaism, it would lead to power struggles and diminish the word of God. Paul disagreed with that idea. Paul spoke about the need for what he called "overseers" of the Church. A big problem for Paul was that he was not the only person creating a new religion. Today, the United Methodist church uses the phrase "an expression of Christianity" to explain why inside of the denomination, there are churches that are not following the rules and regulations of the organization. They are being called expressions of Methodism. Well, in the years after the resurrection, there were several expressions of Christianity emerging.

Paul wanted his expression of Jesus Christ to win the day. Therefore, he created the Episcopal (derived from the Greek word for overseer) system for his new house churches. This united the house churches and gave this new organization, called the Proto-Orthodox Church, the power it needed to fight the other Christian expressions. History clearly states that the Proto-orthodox won the battle for the expression of Christianity. The new church organization naturally said that it was the only expression of Christianity that Jesus wanted. It won the battle, so why not take a victory lap?

The newly founded Church was immediately placed in a position of having to defend itself from the Roman government. The Roman Empire killed many converts to the Christian faith. However, in 311 CE, Constantine made Christianity a legal religion in his territories. By 318 CE, when he became the emperor, he legalized Christianity and made it the religion of the Roman Empire.

The small house churches turned into enormous churches overnight. Constantine allowed the growing church to use government buildings called basilicas as their new buildings. Christian gained millions of converts overnight. The Church, with its Pope and bishops, gained a huge amount of power. Its hierarchy allowed it to gain power. When the Roman Empire fell around 425 CE with the invasion of the Visigoths, a power vacuum was created, and the Church stepped in and took control. The Church in the Dark Ages was the government. It had power over millions of people, both religiously and as the government.

The Church maintained its power throughout the Dark Ages and through the Middle Ages. Its control was dampened with the emergence of nationalism. As the new countries formed, the Church lost some of its power. However, the Pope still held a great deal of power. Even kings and queens would bow to the wishes of the Pope in Rome. Of course, I am referring to the Catholic Church, which held western

Europe under its influence. The same thing was happening in Eastern Europe as the Orthodox church helped onto its power.

Today, the Church does not have the same power over nations. The concept of Christendom ended in the 1960s everywhere. In the United States, the blue laws that prohibited businesses to be open on Sunday were eliminated, breaking the last tie between Church and state. The proper separation in the United States of Church and state was done. Today, the government ignores the Church. As fewer people are a part of the Church, the less power that it will have to influence government.

At the local level, there have always been and always will be parishioners who crave the power of controlling other people. The local churches have a hierarchical system that allows a few to dictate the rules of the Church to the rest of the body. It is a part of human nature to create organizations. With organizations comes the need for leadership. With leadership comes corruption and so on. Every Church has a political system that developed over time and will always exist. The power base in the Church determines how the Church will be presented as the Church of Jesus Christ. Sometimes it is hard to find Jesus in the Church because of the layers of politics and power.

The Pilgram Found Jesus

It is hard for a pilgrim to find Jesus in the Church today. The history of the Church hangs around its neck, making it difficult to see Jesus. But the pilgrim can find Jesus once the pilgrim is aware of the layers that must be peeled. Think about an onion for a moment. It has layers, a lot of layers. It is the core that the pilgrim is looking for. The Church is like an onion because of the layers that must be peeled back to find the center. It is Jesus who is in the center. It is difficult to remove the layers, but it is vital to do so.

So, what did this pilgrim find in the center of the layers of the Church? After over twenty years of searching, my understanding of Jesus is not very complicated. Jesus is my rabbi and teacher who explains God to me. The "passport" into Heaven is understanding that one must love God and love neighbor. That is the message. How do I do this? My rabbi and teacher, Jesus, told me how to do it and showed it. The Gospels are the key to finding Jesus. I have been studying the Gospel, searching for the original meaning of Jesus' words and actions. It has been a significant pilgrimage so far, and I know it will continue to be one. I have discovered the original meaning of Matthew's Gospel (it is available in print and Kindle). At the time of this writing, I am halfway through Mark's Gospel. Then I will examine, and research John's Gospel followed by Luke. Every passage that I study to uncover the original meaning brings me closer to Jesus. The quest will never stop.

Jesus is my Messiah. He is my Messiah because it was through a fundamental understanding of His teaching that brought me back to God. I left God early in life because of circumstances in my family of origin. When I was mentally ready to find the positivism of life and purpose, I found Jesus. His words and actions spoke to me at a rudimentary level. Jesus' words and actions brought me back into the family of God. He is my Messiah because I feel connected to God. I look to Jesus' wisdom when making life decisions. I have received many blessings from heaven through Jesus.

Now I do research to discover the original meaning of God's word, which includes Jesus' words, not only for myself. I have been sharing my research through several avenues. My research papers can be found at my website http://michaelkoplitz.info. You can also find them at academia.edu and researchgate.net. I am thrilled that so many people have been reading the papers. My books are available at any bookseller. For a person who does not advertise, the books are selling. Not huge volumes, but enough to help other pilgrims to find Jesus.

I found Jesus, and I have had 24 years of pastoral ministry where I shared my findings and helped other pilgrims find Jesus. I hope that many more pilgrims will find my writings helpful to them in finding Jesus. I pray that your reading of this book will help you as well.

Your Pilgrimage

Now the remaining point is before you. Are you on a pilgrimage to find Jesus? You may be on the expedition and are having trouble finding Jesus. As you can see, the Church does not make it easy. There are so many traditions and obstacles to overcome. I was not satisfied with the answer the Church gave me when I ask about who Jesus is. Do not be happy with the basic response. Here it is; "Jesus saves you from Hell because He died for the forgiveness of your sins." That is an excellent statement, but for me, it did not tell me much about Jesus. In fact, it never answered my question about how a man dying 2000 years ago can offer me salvation.

If you are in this or a similar situation, do not despair. I found Jesus through years of learning and research. You can find your Jesus as well. Remember that your Jesus may differ from another person's Jesus. Remember that you have to make Jesus your own. It is your understanding of who Jesus is that matters. I have taken you on a part of my journey. However, I must admit to you I could not include everything from the journey in one book. I did cover the critical points and obstacles to finding Jesus.

It is your pilgrimage. You can seek out advice on how your journey might progress. Remember that it is YOUR PILGRIMAGE and not anyone else's. Who knows what treasures you will find on your travels? I offer a prayer that you have a time of discovery on your journey. If you think I can help, you can reach me through my website. I will help other pilgrims as much as I can. Jesus called me to learn the original meaning of His words and to preach it to the world. Helping people on their pilgrimage is preaching the word. May God bless you in your travels. Amen.

About this Pilgrim

Website: http://michaelkoplitz.info

You can learn more about me and all my research, education videos, and church videos at this website.

www.ingramcontent.com/pod-product-compliance
Lightning Source LLC
Chambersburg PA
CBHW022018150726

47990CB00002B/710